THE
NEXT GREAT
CRUSADE
OF OUR TIME

Michael P. Wright

The opinions expressed by the author are not necessarily those of Revival Waves of Glory Books & Publishing.

Published by Revival Waves of Glory Books & Publishing
PO Box 596| Litchfield, Illinois 62056 USA
www.revivalwavesofgloryministries.com

Revival Waves of Glory Books & Publishing is committed to excellence in the publishing industry.

Published in the United States of America

Paperback: 978-1-68411-026-1

Hardcover: 978-1-68411-027-8

Table of Contents

A Book Inspired by God.

Perspective by a
United States
Army Green Beret

Author
Michael P. Wright

Those Who Don't Know
History are Condemned to
Repeat it.

Chapter 1:

ORIGINS OF THE CRUSADE – SOVIET UNION INVASION

The surprise invasion of Afghanistan in 1979 by the Soviet Union military shocked many nations. The war started in December 1979 to February 1989 and lasted over nine years. Soviet troops invaded Kabul on order from Moscow to replace Hafizullah Amin with the Soviet endorsed Babrak Karmal as head of the Democratic Republic of Afghanistan. In December 1979 began the first deployment of the army arriving in the capital of Kabul, they staged a coup, killing the Afghan President and installing a rival Afghan socialist.

The Soviet Union's war and occupation of Afghanistan led to a jihad, a holy war in the country. The Mujahidin warriors rose up to fight the Soviet war machine with whatever weapons they had at their disposal. The holy warrior's tactic was to draw the Soviets out of the cities and into the mountainous areas where they had the advantage. Foreign fighters started to stream into Afghanistan and join the fight. The Soviets soon became bogged down and found themselves in an endless war with no easy way out.

America soon started to supply the Mujahidin with modern weapons of war. This became another cold war between America and the Soviet Union, two rival countries. The holy warriors received weapons and training to fight the massive Soviet force which swelled to over one hundred thousand troops. The years went by and the war was fought to a standstill.

Osama Bin Laden received his combat training and expertise in Afghanistan. He became a recognized leader among men. Arab fighters came from all over the Middle East to join the jihad. Pakistan was used as a staging ground for the holy warriors' while they waited for weapons to fight the war. The Mujahidin formed their army in western Pakistan known as the tribal area.

Afghanistan throughout its history has rarely been able to live in peace and has been invaded many times. The origins of the next great crusade between the Christians and Muslims began in Afghanistan in 1979. The Soviet Union had no idea what they got themselves into and what they are responsible for starting. Scholars of history will judge our time and how this invasion began a serious of events that were unstoppable.

During all this fighting the beginning of the Taliban existence came about. Once a jihad is declared there is no easy end in sight and another reason to continue the fight presents itself. In the Arabic viewpoint, the antagonistic western culture can only be tolerated to a certain point. A clash between cultures has happened many times throughout mankind. Unstoppable events from 1979 to this point leading the western and Muslim cultures into a crusade with no end in sight.

A tipping point has occurred with the aggression of the Soviet Union against a neighboring country of Afghanistan. The adventurism of an empire to have more control in the region and dictate its will to other countries has led the world to its present day dilemma.

Chapter 2:
EMBOLDEN THE MUJAHIDIN

After the Soviet Union's withdraw from Afghanistan in 1989, the government collapsed. The country was controlled by the many different tribes and the law was dictated by the tribal elders. The Mujahidin had won a great victory and melted back into their different tribes and areas of the Middle East. Warlords began to take hold of certain areas in the country and their control was absolute. The tribal elders in Afghanistan installed a new central government in Kabul to oversee the country.

The Taliban began to emerge and started taking over areas of the country. Some of the former Mujahidin fighters joined with the Taliban who were striving for a hard-line Islamic state. The new regime grew in strength and capability while taking control of larger territory. The central government was now under direct threat from the Taliban who wouldn't negotiate and were receiving foreign aid to take control of the country.

Osama bin Laden began forming his terrorist training camps in Afghanistan which were becoming more lawless. Bin Laden became a warlord by his own right and had many fighters under his command. He was already on the radar of western intelligence and being watched even closer. This was time for his planning and what he intended to do. Bin Laden was bringing in fighters from different parts of the Middle East and training them for missions around the world. Al-Qaeda and Osama bin Laden would soon become names known to most people. The founder and head of the Islamist militant group which was formed from the Mujahidin had training camps in Afghanistan and Sudan.

During this time alliances were being built with other terrorist networks. Training continued in the relatively safe areas of the mountains of Afghanistan. Communication became a concern with ease dropping on conversations. Soon the use of satellite phones came to an end and messengers were utilized. Also satellite observation by western intelligence had to be dealt with.

Chapter 3:
FIRST GULF WAR

The Gulf War beginning on August 2, 1990 was the next major fight of the Arab jihad. The American military used the code name of Operation Desert Shield and Operation Desert Storm ending on February 28, 1991. The coalition of thirty-four nations was led by the United States in the defense of Saudi Arabia and the removal of Iraqi forces from Kuwait. The largest military alliance since World War II launched an air and naval bombardment for five weeks and then a ground assault which lasted 100 hours. During the fighting, Iraq launched scud missiles at the coalition forces and Israel.

President Sadam Hussein was testing the western nations resolve to see if they had a will to fight. Iraq had just finished fighting a war with Iran for eight years which ended in a cease-fire and Iraq needed a military victory. Iraq had considered Kuwait to be their territory and would do what was necessary to take control of it. Iraq was also a state sponsor of terrorism which was often directed towards Israel.

The Arab jihad would continue even though Iraq lost the war. The coalition of nations entered and held the border areas of Iraq for a short time before they withdrew. President Sadam Hussein remained in power and started to rebuild Iraq's military for any future war. The chemical weapons that Iraq possessed continued to be a severe concern for the region. The United Nations warnings to President Sadam Hussein were ignored by him and his commanders. The international community would need to stand strong against Iraq and monitor all of their military actions. Iraq had a few allies mostly terrorist states to help them.

The country began to rearm for any future aggression and continued to supply terrorist groups with weapons. Sanctions were still in place to slow down Iraq's economy. Iraq was still producing chemical weapons to be used as a deterrent to any future aggression. Oil production throughout the country was at its peak to supply all the money necessary for the military.

Chapter 4:
EMBASSY BOMBINGS AND U.S.S. COLE

Terror struck East Africa at the United States embassies in Kenya and Tanzania on August 7, 1998 when nearly simultaneous truck bombs exploded and killed 224 people. This was a revenge attack for various reasons which include the invasion of Somalia by the U.S. military and Saudi Arabia allowing U.S. troops into their country before the start of the first Gulf War. Al-Qaeda and Osama bin Laden were responsible for the attack and for the first time America was introduced to the terrorist network by mass media. The jihad, holy war against the west would continue on by striking at U.S. facilities around the world. Osama bin Laden's long-term goal was to lure the United States into Afghanistan which is known as the graveyard of empires. In response to the embassy bombings cruise missile strikes were ordered on targets in Sudan and Afghanistan including terrorist training camps.

The USS Cole bombing was a terrorist attack against a U.S. Navy guided missile destroyer on October 12, 2000. It was attacked while in the harbor and being refueled in the Yemeni port of Aden. A small boat carrying explosives and two suicide bombers approached the side of the destroyer and exploded. Seventeen American sailors were killed and thirty-nine were injured in the incident. It was a routine refueling stop with no hostilities in the area. This attack happened one year before September 11, 2001 and it was meant to show that any American assets were not safe. Al-Qaeda boldly claimed responsibility for the attack.

Al-Qaeda previously attempted a similar attack on the U.S. Navy destroyer USS The Sullivans while in the same port on January 3, 2000. The plot was the same to load a small boat full of explosives and detonate it near the side of the destroyer. The small boat was overloaded and it sank before it could complete its task. The U.S. Navy learned a valuable lesson from this experience and how to better protect its ships. Many resources came to the aid of the USS Cole for protection and temporary repairs.

Chapter 5:
SEPTEMBER 11, 2001
– THE BEGINNING

From my own perspective of the events that happened that day. It started out as any other day and by the morning disaster struck which changed the world forever. I was watching television that day on a large screen and turned to ABC news with Peter Jennings, God rest his soul. What I saw next was truly shocking to see one of the World Trade Center buildings on fire and that a plane had struck the building. At that point, it wasn't believed to be an attack just an accident. There was a lot of speculation being reported as to how this happened. Emergency crews from the fire department were starting to respond and enter the building. Flames were pouring out of the broken windows high above around the ninetieth floor and rising up the building. It was horrifying to watch as people were standing in the windows trying to escape the intense heat. Then all of a sudden one person jumps out and then several others also jump. It is very difficult to understand what was going through their minds unless we were put into a similar circumstance.

Then all of a sudden a second passenger plane slammed into the other twin tower with a tremendous explosion and fireball. The Pentagon also had a passenger plane fly right into it and it was the same section of the Pentagon which just had a renovation done to it. What was taking place on the morning of September 11, 2001 is enough to shake a person to their core. Later that morning it was found out that a fourth passenger plane had crashed into a field in Pennsylvania. After all the events that took place on that morning, I already knew like many other people did that the United States of America was now at war.

After the fourth passenger plane had crashed and all these planes were being used as weapons of destruction then the government decided to ground all planes. The planes in the air were directed to land at the nearest airport. The tragic events of that morning were still in progress and the responders were attempting to save as many lives as possible.

It was after nine o'clock in the morning then all of a sudden one of the towers started to collapse from the top of the tower and fall cascading into its structure until the entire building collapsed onto the ground below. From the coverage on the television everyone was astonished to see this and on the ground, there was sheer panic. Twenty minutes later the second tower collapsed the same way and then both World Trade Canters were on the ground. At the time it was hard to believe that this had happened and how could it be possible for an attack like this to occur. The wall of dust and debris was blinding and everyone was running for their lives.

America was now deeply involved in the next great crusade of our time against the Muslim attackers and there was no backing down. The rage across America grew quickly and an aggressive response was demanded. There was fear that people were trapped inside the debris of the World Trade Center. Many firefighters were unaccounted for after the collapse and an urgent request for help from all of the surrounding states was sent out. Heavy lifting equipment was brought to the site and firefighters as well as volunteers from states all over the country joined a twenty-four hour rescue operation. Day after day bodies were recovered with the seldom rescue of a trapped individual to bring relief and joy to the rescue crews. After a week went by the rescue operation turned into a recovery operation. Clean up of all the twisted steel and debris started which would be a long and tedious process.

Chapter 6:
REPERCUSSIONS

After the attack, America became more united like in all times before a conflict is about to start. All government agencies and departments improved their security posture. The Congress and Senate made changes in the government with new laws to protect the country from further attack. A new department called Homeland Security was formed at the cost of billions of dollars and with a headquarters location that is classified until today. More than twelve departments are under Homeland Security for stronger command and control.

The FAA had a total security shakedown with many changes that were made that affect everyone today. Personally, I used to enjoy flying and looked forward to taking a flight but now it has unfortunately become a burden. New technology is being implemented in the airports and on board the airplanes to make air travel safer for the public. The long lines that must be endured at the airports for extra security checks are here to stay.

The armed forces of the United States of America started preparing to receive their orders for combat. The targets to strike were being assessed and air power would be essential for the first stages of the attack. Forward bases were being prepared for fighter planes and transport planes. Staging areas for combat troops were being built. America was in full combat mode and getting ready for a massive revenge attack. The country was now furious and ready to pour it onto those responsible for September 11th.

History will judge President Bush's impending actions and whether there were enough combat troops to support his actions. The American public expected and demanded quick retaliation with devastating results. The reality of the situation was about to hit hard onto those who started this war. The full might of the American armed forces was about to be directed at the enemy. The worst attack on America would bring destruction down on top of the attackers.

Chapter 7:

AFGHANISTAN

America began to position its armed forces for a major assault on Afghanistan. Long range bombers and fighter aircraft started to move into the region. Aircraft carriers were positioned for a strike and would be very useful to bring the fight to the enemy. The bombing began with many types of aircraft and cruise missiles from warships targeting all of the training camps and command and control facilities. Heavy bombardment of the mountainous areas to destroy the enemy hideouts had started.

Retribution was at hand with absolutely no sympathy for the enemy. Osama bin Laden was in hiding in the country and most likely in one of the caves he was so familiar with. Intense carpet bombing of the mountains was non-stop to bring to an end America's number one enemy. The followers of Al-Qaida were being annihilated by the hundreds and their training camps were being flattened. The only place to run to was Pakistan and that country's borders were being closely monitored for any activity.

America was taking no prisoners and soon ground troops would arrive in Afghanistan to take the fight to the enemy. U.S. armed forces poured into the country and soon took control of the government. The areas outside of the cities were lawless and controlled by the tribes which are where the fighting was happening. A modern mechanized army against local tribesman and terrorists should be an easy victory for the strongest military in the world. But it was not to be and America found itself in the longest war of its history which is still continuing today. Afghanistan has a long history of outlasting many invaders into its country and the tribesman know the terrain very well which they use to their advantage.

Chapter 8:
IRAQ BUILDUP

The next great crusade would continue on with the preparation for the next military invasion of another Muslim country. One army and marine division after another were brought into Kuwait for staging to attack. More U.S. Naval aircraft carrier groups were once again steaming quickly to the gulf region. Long range bombers and fighter aircraft were already in position and on standby. The assets of the American military are tremendous and it was about to be demonstrated.

Other countries were sending in military units to join in the fight. What President Herbert Walker Bush started on August 2, 1990, President George Bush would finish more than ten years later. President Sadam Hussein of Iraq would not follow the directives of the United Nations after the first Gulf War and believed he could do whatever he wanted. Iraq's military had already been rebuilt and was ready to repel an invading army. Once again Iraq's government was wrong and was facing a coalition thou not as large as their first Gulf War.

America's coalition was growing larger by the week and was training for an invasion with every unit being assigned objectives. This attack was meant to shock and awe the enemy into an early surrender. The Iraqi government was given an ultimatum to stand-down which they ignored and the military thought it had the capacity to stop an attack. The Elite Republican Guard claimed they were prepared to stop an invasion of their country. No Arabic country had ever experienced a military assault of this magnitude that was about to happen.

Chapter 9:
IRAQ INVASION

The U.S. military was more than ready to unleash its fury and planned to move quickly through the country of Iraq. The chemical weapons in the country would need to be secured before an assault could happen. The shock and awe that Iraq was warned about would soon start. The beginning of the attack took place in the early morning hours with a tremendous onslaught of firepower reigning down on the enemy. After the bombing had its effect, the military units started to move into the country with the U.S. Marines up front. The Iraqi military was facing the most powerful army in the world and would do what they had to in order to defend their country.

Many American military divisions started moving throughout the country engaging Iraqi units one after another. Swiftly the country was being overrun by U.S. forces and Iraq was overmatched. Coalition forces had their role and assigned objectives of engagement. President Sadam Hussein wanted a jihad against the invaders but his army was pushed back and on the run. A crusade of western and European powers fighting a Muslim country was repeating in history again. The attack raged on and the cities fell one by one into coalition control. The Iraqi army started to fall apart with soldiers removing their uniforms and melting into the civilian population.

The fighting was coming to an end with isolated pockets of resistance. The top commanders went into hiding for self-preservation and a possibility of fighting another day. The political leaders fled the capital and others snuck out of the country. Sadam Hussein's sons were killed in a standoff with the U.S. military and the president of Iraq went into the countryside to hide. Coalition forces led by the American military seized control of the country very quickly. Casualties were lower than expected because of the exceptional training of the coalition armies. The Iraqi military was well equipped and motivated but was lacking in training.

Chapter 10:
OCCUPATION

The war came to an end quickly and hundreds of thousands of American forces occupied Iraq. Zones were set up in the country for control of the green zone being the most secure. The hunt was on to find high priority generals and politicians. A deck of cards with individuals' faces was used as a tool to locate these targets. Mostly it was successful in locating these high-priority individuals. Base camps were set up in the country for security of the troops and equipment. Some camps were used as interrogation centers for enemy combatants and terrorists. Useful intelligence was gained to stop further attacks and protect coalition forces.

A new Iraqi government was formed and protected to give it a chance to succeed. Iraq was entering a new era of its history and only the people could make it succeed. The government needed to gain new international links and still does. Iraq has a long history dating back to ancient times but could the country adapt to the new reality. The economy of the country needed to be rebuilt and brought back up and running. The Iraqi economy is dependent on oil for the country's survival. Many oil facilities needed major repairs and new equipment to operate properly. America was helping Iraq to reposition itself and to become independent again.

The occupation continued on with the trial of Sadam Hussein for his past atrocities'. He had a lot to account for with his behavior towards the people of Iraq. It is his responsibility for the long drawn out Iran and Iraq war that killed hundreds of thousands. He is responsible for using chemical weapons against Kurdish civilians and killing thousands of innocent people. It is his responsibility for invading Kuwait because of his lust for power and greediness. With all of this Iraq was also a state sponsor of terrorism which Sadam Hussein had to answer for. These are some of the major charges against him which had to be proved in a court of law. The outcome of the trial was final and the verdict was hanging in the gallows until death.

Chapter 11:
TERRORIST VIOLENCE

The remnants of the Iraqi army started attacking coalition forces through terrorist violence. It was a matter of getting even for the invading forces taking control of the country. Many different tactics were used in the violence including IED, booby traps, and car bombs. The activity was non-stop and it was more than harassment to drive out the coalition forces. There would be no peace in Iraq until the invading forces were pushed out of the country. This had turned into unconventional warfare with many civilians being killed in the explosions. The country had turned into total chaos with very few safe havens to take refuge in.

Coalition patrols were sent out daily and protected as much as possible while not knowing where the next attack would come from. Many casualties happened every month with no chance of many of the injured ever returning to the battlefield. The injuries were so severe and disabling even the hardest veterans used extreme caution when in the field. Many of these IED are not powerful enough to destroy armored vehicles but the bombs cause death and crippling injuries with loss of single or multiple limbs. To see their comrades' loose arms and legs is very agonizing and demoralizing. It is enough to keep many soldiers from reenlisting and get out of military service altogether. This is exactly what these terrorists want and the soldiers that stay in the service find themselves serving multiple years in a war zone with many serving up to four to five years.

This terrorist violence went on for several years and became a daily grind for coalition forces. Tremendous effort to find these bomb makers through military intelligence and interrogation happened every day. Some of these bomb makers were located and many others weren't. Valuable intelligence was gained through the ones that were found and leading to other arrests. Seeking and finding these people became crucial to saving lives and stopping injuries of coalition forces. The root of this problem had to be cut out and that meant finding the planners behind these destructive bombs.

Chapter 12:
SECTARIAN FIGHTING

The terrorist violence led to sectarian fighting between the Sunnis and Shia. The situation in Iraq turned into tribal warfare for control of the country. These ancient tribal loyalties run deep and in times of trouble the country can become divided. The sectarian differences have the power to change the political alliances and structure in the country. The struggle for dominating territory in Iraq is the main factor in the outcome. Throughout history, the two tribal factions have had conflicts with each other and many times ending in a truce.

The fighting between the two rival tribes is respectful and doesn't target families as well as religious sites. For centuries the tribes have lived side by side with both having their own responsibilities to control the country. The Sunnis and Shia can live in peace and have done so for long periods of time. There are certain elements that take advantage of that peace and draw both sides into conflict as well as an uncertain future. Harmony in the country becomes elusive and fighting rages on bringing the country into a civil war. Starting a war is easy but trying to reach an end result and bring a war to an end is more than challenging.

Other countries in the region watch the situation in Iraq and look for an opening to send in weapons for a profit and possibly sending in their own troops. As far as the western countries are concerned and the coalition forces they will all stay out of the fighting to see where it leads to. The hostilities continued back and forth with no major changes in the country just more casualties. Territory shifted between both sides with the oil wells being the prize. The real power in the country was the U.S. Army which was doing its best to hold the country together. The Iraqi government had collapsed leaving a huge power vacuum and once the tribal fighting had stopped the government would need to be rebuilt.

Chapter 13:
U.S. ARMY SURGE

With the continuing civil war in the country, the U.S. Army needed a stronger presence to bring the country under control. The American military manpower swelled inside Iraq while being able to monitor larger territories in the country. More equipment and armored personnel carriers were brought in as well as air support. With close to two-hundred thousand troops in Iraq, there was speculation that the U.S. Army was preparing to invade another country in the region. The western crusade in the Middle East was in full force and there was no stopping it. The politicians in Washington, D.C. had their plans all laid out and ready to implement. At this point, total control of strategic countries in the Middle East was very tempting.

The surge of troops in the country put a wedge between the Sunnis and Shia to slow down the fighting. Once control was reached the two rivals would be convinced to come to the negotiating table. It was a struggle to bring calm into the country and all the indiscriminate bombings would need to come to an end. Increased patrols throughout the cities were taking place to show a strong presence and not give any potential terrorists a chance to place any bombs in public areas. The patrols went out every day to change the situation and find out any intelligence that could be gained. The strategy was working and businesses were reopening to bring some kind of normalcy to Iraq.

The coalition forces were receiving cooperation from the community to stop the terrorist attacks. Over time the situation improved and less IED were being placed in market areas and in busy intersections. The interaction with the elders was getting better and more information was being shared. The objectives of the coalition forces were being realized and the violence was coming to an end. Negotiations between the Sunnis and Shia started happening and everyone was striving for a quick end to this conflict. Fewer patrols were being sent into public areas and the base camps were kept secure from any potential terrorist attacks.

Chapter 14:
UNIT DOWNSIZING

Plans were being finalized for the American military to downsize units and to start sending personnel back to the U.S. More than thirty thousand troops needed to be sent back to the bases in the U.S. Also all of their equipment, base material, and armored personnel carriers needed to go back. This was a major undertaking and many military transport flights would need to take place. Some of these troops would be rotated into Afghanistan to replace other military personnel. Even though unit downsizing was taking place in Iraq there were still multiple tours of duty for personnel happening in Iraq and Afghanistan. There were no easy answers to solve this problem and PSD is a very common disorder with troops returning to the U.S.

This realignment of troops would take many months to accomplish and the cost was significant. The reduction of personnel in the country was happening and the usual routine of daily patrols would eventually be back to normal again. The situation in Iraq had changed for the better with calm in the market places and in the busy intersections. The Sunnis and Shia had come to an understanding and an agreement. Both tribes would cooperate to form a new government to represent everyone in the country. Iraq was having a fresh beginning after many decades of Sadam Hussein in power and having his own way.

The Sunnis and Shia councils would need to agree on the president and officials for Iraq. It is very difficult to have an election in a country that has been ravaged by war. The new government was appointed and put into position with a tremendous amount of work ahead of them. They had daunting responsibilities to accomplish to rebuild Iraq which had been devastated by war. The whole country was counting on the new president and officials to bring change to the country. An outpouring of support was needed from all the concerned countries to reconstruct many buildings and bridges in all of the major cities of Iraq. The country has never experienced anything like this type of destruction of its structures.

Chapter 15:
U.S. ARMY WITHDRAW

The new Iraqi government was in place with a functioning council that was ready to direct the country to its future. The country was becoming stronger and more stable with a new military that was under training. It would take years to prepare adequately untrained recruits for modern warfare. The Iraqi military needed to rearm with modern weapons and learn how to use them. The U.S. government started supplying weapons of all types to the Iraqi military. American military trainers were very busy training the new military recruits. The untested soldiers started going out on patrols under the watchful eyes of the American trainers.

The new military was progressing and growing quickly reaching one-hundred thousand troops under training. The U.S. Army was planning and preparing to start withdrawing from Iraq. Over one-hundred and fifty thousand troops would need to be withdrawn and could Iraq stand on their own which was the main concern. After many years of the American military fighting in Iraq from 2003 – 2011 and too many casualties, it was time for the U.S. to get out. The President of the United States was under political pressure to withdraw the American military from Iraq. After eight years of constant fighting and IED bomb attacks, the U.S. Army was ready to move out.

The day arrived when the U.S. military started to withdraw unit by unit in a gradual pull out. The separation was done in phases and a section of the country at a time. Organization and paying attention to detail was the only way to accomplish the task at hand. A withdrawing military is very vulnerable to attack and full protection was in place as well as air support. The equipment with vehicles of all types including tanks and helicopters were loaded onto transport ships ready to be sent back to bases in the U.S. The troops were sent back on transport planes and commercial air carriers.

Chapter 16:
WAR IN SYRIA

Now we are up to the present time and the ongoing fighting in Syria which is one of the oldest countries in the world dating back to ten thousand years ago. The civil war in Syria began March 15, 2011 just about five years ago which began with anti-government protests. More than two-hundred and fifty-thousand Syrians have lost their lives in the armed conflict. There are over fourteen million Syrians that are now refugees spread around neighboring countries and some are now in European countries. Syria only has a total population of fewer than twenty-three million people. This is the largest refugee crisis since World War II and it is a human disaster as well as an international crisis.

Basher al-Assad the president of Syria is very responsible for this crisis because he refuses to negotiate with his own people. The president is following the same path as his father did but his father was able to crush the opposition. Bashar al-Assad has too many enemies against him which are the Free Syrian Army, the Kurdish Army, and ISIS. Bashar al-Assad days are numbered and he won't last much longer. The Syrian government and Syrian opposition are preparing to meet a United Nations envoy in Geneva with a goal of ending the war. It is believed Bashar al-Assad is living in a bubble and detached from what is happening in his country. He is fully protected by his political aids which do whatever his is and he has security all around him so he can't be touched. Bashar al-Assad will ultimately be held accountable for exactly what has happened to the Syrians and the country which does not belong to him.

Syria no longer has a border with Iraq because the country is overrun with enemies. When peace finally comes to Syria there is still the problem with the Kurdish Army, which wants its own state and ISIS which wants to create a caliphate in Syrian and Iraqi territory. Syria will need to replace Bashar al-Assad and the new president will need to unite the country against all their enemies. Saudi Arabia is with the Syrian opposition and will undoubtedly help them to rearm and possibly training for the troops. Syria will need international help to destroy ISIS and the best way to defeat them is with infantry, tanks, and air support. Bombing ISIS positions are not enough to defeat them but it does slow down their progress.

Chapter 17:
RISE OF ISIS

Why did this happen? I will tell you why because people can only be pushed so far and then they reach their limit. The U.S. military and intelligence agencies have tortured and mistreated many Arabs in prisons across the countries of Iraq and Afghanistan. In ISIS point of view, to put it bluntly, there is going to be hell to pay and they defiantly mean just that. ISIS wants their revenge through an extremist jihad targeting Christians and Arabs as they fight to establish their caliphate. This is their crusade against the western powers and their influence reaches around the world. ISIS uses many ways to recruit young Arabs to their cause and using social media is their most common tool. The group has a tremendous following of disenfranchised young Arab males.

These young men are now involved in a revolving door of military training, combat, and then returning to their home country to form terrorist cells for attacks against civilians and the government. I believe the day will come when there will be a major uprising of young Arab combat veterans in many western countries if the present situation does not change. I totally blame America for what is happening right now in the Middle East and there is no doubt who started these agonizing events. The world is now in a modern crusade of Christian nations against Arab nations. We see the surface of this problem but what lies underneath can be deceiving. It is believed that many of the Arab countries that support what the western countries are doing in the Middle East also financially support ISIS. So who is the real enemy here? Time will tell as it always does.

The world has fallen into a crusade and a war on terrorism that is affecting most countries. Terrorism has been around for thousands of years but now it has reached a new level. A major revenge attack for Osama bin Laden who was killed a short time ago, only five years has passed since then, has not taken place yet. There is absolute and hostile anger for how Osama bin Laden was killed in Pakistan. I believe September 11, 2001 was just a precursor to what is coming and the next attack will be devastating. A possible chemical or biological attack in a closed area such as a crowded subway station could happen. ISIS has the resources to purchase a small nuclear device which is not out of their reach and it could be detonated in a large city in the U.S. causing maximum damage and destruction.

Chapter 18:
MIDDLE EAST ON FIRE

The whole world is watching the turmoil that is happening in Iraq, Syria and Afghanistan. The region of the Middle East is on fire with a danger of dragging more countries into the conflict. ISIS is on the march and their constantly recruiting from all over the Middle East, North Africa, and many western countries. ISIS lure is powerful and inspires the youth to join while offering large amounts of money as well as automobiles. They have turned into a mercenary army using Muslim extremism as a calling. ISIS is well funded, organized, moderately trained, and not afraid to die. That is right, not afraid to die and you can't say that about well trained western soldiers.

There is no longer a border between Iraq and Syria. The territory now belongs to ISIS and they will take more ground if they are not aggressively confronted. If ISIS keeps expanding they will eventually control most of Iraq and Syria. Then the group will start targeting other countries in the region such as Jordan and Turkey. Terrorist attacks have already happened in these two countries and ISIS ultimately wants the entire region under their control.

The group wants to establish a caliphate in the Middle East and will do whatever it takes including slaughtering as many Christians and Muslims as they deem necessary. Some of Sadam Hussein's ex-military officers are in command of ISIS forces and as far as their concerned there will be repercussions for what has happened in the past.

There are different acronyms to describe this group with different meanings. ISIL which is Islamic State of Iraq and the Levant. ISIS which is Islamic State of Iraq and Syria or Islamic State of Iraq and al-Sham. This group is a salafi jihadist militant group that follows an Islamic fundamentalist Wahhabi doctrine of Sunni Islam.

Abu Bakr al-Baghdadi is in military command of ISIL or ISIS and is also a spiritual leader. ISIL or ISIS follows a distinctive variety of Islam whose beliefs about the path to the Day of Judgment matters to its strategy. The black flag of ISIL or ISIS is more than just a flag with Arabic writing on it because the flag represents death.

Chapter 19:

COALITION AGAINST ISIS

The coalition against ISIS has more than sixty countries worldwide that are involved in it with western and Islamic countries. Thirty-four Islamic nations have formed a coalition to fight terrorism. There are many nations prepared to stand up against ISIS and put a stop to their rampage. Some of these nations have been directly attacked by ISIS causing them to join the coalition. Other nations have had military personnel killed by ISIS prompting them to join. An example is that one nation had an air force pilot's plane that was shot down and then the pilot was put on display inside a cage while shortly after that he was burned to death. This enraged Abdullah II bin Al-Hussein of Jordan also known as King Abdullah II of Jordan who has trained as an air force pilot as well. King Abdullah II believes ISIS can be defeated quickly which he had made clear. His air force has bombed ISIS positions many times for retribution.

The country of Turkey is also involved in air strikes against ISIS because of attacks in its country. Iran is providing limited troops under the command of an Iranian general to fight ISIS in Iraq. Old enemies are co-operating together to defeat a very troubling threat. The United Arab Emirates is actively bombing ISIS positions in Syria and the first country to have a female pilot flying missions into Syria. There are many other Arab nations that are standing up against ISIS and they realize that this group and its behavior can't be tolerated. Ultimately the Arab nations together will defeat ISIS. Air power alone will not be enough to defeat ISIS and infantry as well as tank divisions will be needed to finally stop this group's barbaric behavior.

Many European nations are involved in this coalition and providing support. America is certainly in the fight to put an end to ISIS and this group can't be just contained they must be eliminated. One of the ways to slow this group down is to take away their financial resources. Oil wells have come under control of ISIS and they are profiting considerably while selling much of this oil on the black market. These oil wells need to be seized from ISIS and taken control of by the coalition. If the oil wells can't be taken then they must be destroyed. Recently a bank that is controlled by ISIS was destroyed along with the money being held in that bank. This is the way to send a powerful message to the leader of ISIS that their financial resources are being hunted down. This is also exactly what is happening to the leader of ISIS, he is being hunted and eventually he will be found and dealt with. This group has already committed serious war crimes and the day will come when those responsible will be held accountable.

Chapter 20:
COALITION GROWING

Another country recently attacked by ISIS is Indonesia in the capital city of Jakarta and it was very close to the presidential palace. This group is growing quickly throughout the country with signs of its presence in many cities and outer areas. Other terrorist attacks in Indonesia are imminent and it could happen at any time. The Indonesian military force is huge and so is the police force. The Indonesian Special Forces unit 88 is moving all around the country and is engaging and apprehending terrorist suspects wherever they can find them. So far over two-thousand suspects have been arrested and new arrests are happening every day.

ISIS is using Indonesia for recruiting purposes being it is the largest Muslim country in the world. Currently over three-hundred Indonesians are in training in Syria and the government of Indonesia knows who these people are and won't let them reenter the country. I believe ISIS has made a tactical mistake by attacking and recruiting in Indonesia. The largest Muslim country in the world will be ISIS undoing. As I stated, Indonesia has a huge military and it is only a matter of time until it is used effectively against ISIS. The first action by the Indonesian police and military is that every terrorist suspect in Indonesia is being hunted down and arrested. Indonesian society has a culture of minding everyone's business which benefits the authorities to finding these suspects and dealing with them. I know about Indonesian culture and their habits because I have lived in this country since May of 2008. ISIS activities will be stopped in Indonesia and most likely Indonesia will work with the Philippine government to root out terrorist suspects from that country. This will only be the beginning of Indonesia's involvement against ISIS. I anticipate this country will participate in hunting down terrorist suspects throughout South East Asia.

Three countries have committed to sending ground forces into Syria which are Saudi Arabia, Bahrain, and The United Arab Emirates (UAE). This has not happened yet and I believe all three countries are waiting for the right time. The best scenario is for all these countries to fight against ISIS together and as one military force together it is less likely there will be any interference from the Syrian military forces. As I stated before infantry, tank divisions, assault helicopters, and fighter aircraft support will be needed to put an end to ISIS rampage in the Middle

East. Other countries will pay attention to what these three countries are about to do and hopefully, Turkey and Jordan will send in military forces as well. I believe Iraq will support foreign military intervention in their country to fight ISIS and defeat them. This fight in Syria and Iraq against ISIS is an Arab fight and this is one reason why the western nations won't send in ground forces. All the Arab nations want is to live in peace just like all of us.

Chapter 21:
ISIS RECRUITING WORLDWIDE

The recruiting activities of ISIS have become an international calamity affecting the youth of the world. Our youth as we know are very susceptible and impressionable to new ideas. ISIS is using all forms of social media to entice teenagers and young adults to their group. Slick advertising campaigns with flashy websites are being used to lure in the young. It is easy for ISIS to recruit the disenfranchised around the world especially the youth who can't find any job to make money. The youth is told promises of money, vehicles, a new life and a better way of living. Once they are brought into the group, then they are brainwashed and put through a military training program. The ones that don't want to cooperate are most likely executed and their relatives will never know what happened to them. This is the reality of ISIS and how they treat their recruits.

ISIS is recruiting from all over the Arab nations, North Africa, Eastern Europe, and Western Europe. Now Southeast Asia has become their recruiting target with mainly the Philippines and Indonesia to choose from. ISIS will go after other countries in the region to recruit from. Countries need to take an active role to stop this recruiting and participate together to bring this to an end. Governments around the world can work together with internet companies to take down these recruiting websites and do what is necessary to cancel the accounts of people who recruit on social media. Governments need to stop the financing and recruiting for ISIS no matter what it takes and by whatever means.

ISIS is focusing on developing a global network and having access to a huge selection of recruits whenever there needed. After the recruits go through military training with ISIS and fight for as many years as there needed then they are sent back to their home country to await further orders from ISIS. Once there in their home country, they can form cells and prepare for terrorist attacks. So now many countries have combat veterans that are now in waiting for the order to strike at targets chosen by ISIS. These veterans blend into society and get jobs and lead a normal life as much as possible.

Chapter 22:
APPEAL AND WORLD ATTACKS OF ISIS

For some of these youth they believe they are going on an adventure with ISIS and some believe it is a dream come true. Something new is always exciting for the youth. ISIS has launched terrorist attacks on many cities in the world with different effects. One of the most powerful and deadly attacks was recently in Paris which caused great anguish and sorrow. The French air force responded quickly by attacking ISIS positions in Raqqa, Syria and bombing their headquarters. As of this writing, the last terrorist attack was in Jakarta, Indonesia with low casualties and all five terrorists killed by security forces. The Indonesian military and police responded in force by arresting more than two-thousand terrorist suspects and this is still an ongoing effort.

ISIS recently has been forced to establish a new headquarters along Libya's Mediterranean coast after its headquarters in Syria was constantly bombed by Western airstrikes. A two-hundred kilometer area of Libya's coast was seized by ISIS for this purpose. There ISIS is planning its next terrorist attack and it is very possible it could be Russia because of its bombing campaign of ISIS positions and Russia's support of the Syrian government. Russia has now become the most important ally of the Syrian government and will keep President Assad in power. If Russia is attacked by terrorists then the risk of ISIS provoking Russia into an all-out war in Syria is extremely high. President Putin is fully capable to ordering over one-hundred thousand troops into Syria. It is believed that President Putin wants to save the Christians in Syria and Iraq from being totally slaughtered by ISIS and therefore preventing genocide.

If ISIS wants to cause Armageddon in the Middle East, it will have its own private destruction if the Russian armed forces are ordered to attack in strength. Russian armored columns will go right through ISIS positions and surround them on many fronts. The Russian military has come into Syria to intimidate ISIS and it is working well. It seems like the Russian government is setting up ISIS for a major assault and they are just waiting for the right opportunity to attack in force. This will completely change the situation in Syria and Iraq and just maybe President Putin will be regarded as a hero in the Middle East. The Western nations don't want to save the Arab nations from ISIS and now it is up to the Russian government to do so.

Chapter 23:
ROGUE ATTACKS
– LONE WOLF

Rogue attacks are happening in many cities around the world with deadly consequences. These attacks are being done by lone wolves who are unpredictable and are difficult to monitor. What compels individuals to take action and shoot total strangers or to detonate bombs in a crowded area without any regard for human life? There are many reasons why people do this and one common reason is how individuals have been treated by others. A major tragedy or aggravation in someone's life can set them on a path of deadly revenge. We have seen these attacks over and over again in the past years.

These are mainly Muslim attacks against western targets because these individuals are enraged over how the Muslims have been treated throughout the world especially after September 11, 2001. Now it has turned into deep rooted hatred with no forgiveness possible. While the western nations continue to attack Muslim countries this just infuriates the Muslim population. Let us not forget there are over one billion Muslims in this world and tolerance only goes so far. God forbid there are any attacks on Mecca or Medina because if it happens, then the whole situation in the world will explode.

The world seems to be locked into a pattern of hostility with no end in sight. It is easy to start a conflict but to finish it and find peace is very challenging. With the continuing cycle of individuals involved in combat training, fighting in a war, and then returning to their home country to await further orders from ISIS to conduct terrorist attacks in their own country has turned into a nightmare situation for many western nations. It appears some of these individual rogue attacks are carried out by people who are not willing to wait for orders and push forward with their own agenda. After these individual attacks, they are praised by ISIS regardless if they are under orders.

Chapter 24:

DEFENSE AGAINST THE LONE WOLF

The intelligence agencies all over the world are monitoring land lines, handphones, cell phones, satellite phones, text messages, sms messages, the internet, emails, websites, social media, chat rooms, and the list goes on and on. Super computers are being used to decipher encrypted messages over the internet and all types of information coming into countries and going out of countries are being monitored for any terrorist activities. All mass media information is being scrutinized by these super computers to find any links to terrorism. This is happening in many countries that can afford these types of computers.

The lone wolf attack could happen anywhere and at any time. Many cities have multiple cameras monitoring the busiest areas for anything that might be out of place including packages or backpacks left unattended. All police agencies are extra vigilant for any and all types of strange behavior. Worldwide airport passenger screening has increased to a high level of suspicion and everyone is treated as a suspect. Most people used to enjoy air travel and now

I don't believe that is true anymore. It seems our privileges as airline passengers are being taken away from us all in the name of passenger safety. The airlines say this is for our benefit and protection. In these times that we are living in we all have to make sacrifices so nothing will harm us.

Truck bombs and car bombs have not been used in western countries for quite some time. To protect individuals and buildings from these types of attacks is very difficult. Suicide bombers present a whole different problem which the western countries haven't experienced yet. Intelligence services have to protect their citizens against these nightmare scenarios and this is a daunting task. It seems these days everyone needs to be watching and paying attention to their surroundings as well as anticipate what someone else may be up to. This is what our world has come to until we can find a way to live in peace with our fellow man and woman.

Chapter 25:

WHY HAS IT COME TO THIS?

Why has it come to this indeed? Think of the terminology of cause and effect and miscalculation. When President George Bush gave the order to invade Iraq it seemed it was the proper course of action at the time but the consequences of his actions turned out to be unpredictable. It led to extreme sectarian violence between the Sunni and Shia. Then ISIS took control of a major part of the country and the border between Iraq and Syria doesn't exist anymore. President Bush said, "That history will judge his actions", that is for certain. America did not finish what they started and pulled out of Iraq too early and ISIS was just waiting for the right moment to move their forces into Iraq.

Another situation affecting the Middle East is the Arab Spring which started after President Obama gave a motivational speech in Egypt. Soon after his speech, there were protests in Tunisia which spread quickly throughout the Middle East. Egypt and Libya were then affected by the protests and soon after Syria was affected by the protests which led to a civil war. Jordan had protests and King Hussein was able to help his people with their grievances. There are two men who are solely responsible for what has happened in the Middle East and I have already stated their names. History judges everyone and their actions they take. It is time to put blame where it is due.

Realize millions of lives that have been affected in the last fourteen years of conflict in the Middle East and Afghanistan as well as the lives affected by the Arab Spring. All of these millions of people who have been forced to flee their homes for safety because of war and their lives have been totally disrupted and forever changed. Many people have nothing to go back to with their communities devastated and destroyed. God only knows how many innocent civilians have perished and how many soldiers have died fighting wars in these regions. God's prayer for the souls of the innocent and soldiers who have passed away, in Jesus name.

CHAPTER 26:
CRUSADE OF THE 21ST CENTURY

The third crusade of the 12th century from 1187 to 1198 between the holy crusaders of King Richard the Lionheart of England and the holy Muslim warriors of Saladin was a classic battle between Christians and Muslims for control of Jerusalem. Saladin spent ten years fighting and killing Muslims to consolidate his power which is similar to what ISIS is doing right now to consolidate their power. After Saladin consolidated his power he had a vision to retake Jerusalem and put it back under Muslim control. After ISIS consolidates their power, they intend to do the same and retake Jerusalem and put it back under Muslim control. Saladin succeeded over eight-hundred years ago and ISIS expects to do the same.

History is about to repeat itself except now it is on a whole new level and it could turn into a blood bath. Israel has one of the most well trained and well-equipped militaries in the world with over two-hundred nuclear weapons at their disposal. The Israeli military is much stronger than its regional competition and won't capitulate. The Israeli defense forces are ranked sixth in the world and have the most powerful military in the Middle East. The Israeli military will hold its ground and repel any invading force. This time, Jerusalem won't be sacked and the Israeli's are God's chosen people.

Just maybe Christians and Muslims were never meant to coexist together in this world. Both cultures have been fighting with each other for thousands of years. Only God knows if this is part of His master plan for humanity. It is hard to understand why all this fighting continues on until today with no end in sight. With both religions and different cultures mixing together but we still can't live together in peace and harmony. Keeping both religions and cultures isolated in separate countries still won't keep us apart. The question is what will it take to bring both religions into a new existence and new life with each other.

Chapter 27: Brutality of ISIS

The world has not seen this type of brutality since the Middle Ages and it is horrifying to watch as a person is about to be decapitated. During these times we are living in it is very inhumane for this to be happening. ISIS is doing this to intimidate and scare people into submission. Why is God allowing this to happen to so many innocent people? It is unimaginable that this is really taking place in the 21st century. How much longer is mankind going to have to endure this type of behavior and disregard for human life? The longer that this goes on the worse it gets and the death toll keeps rising. All nations living under the rule of law must take responsibility and military action and put a stop to this senseless barbaric activity of ISIS.

ISIS has murdered many Christians and Muslims since their campaign of horror started. ISIS claims that the Muslims they have killed don't have the true faith of Islam. ISIS believes the Christians they have killed are not worthy to live by Muslims and the Christian faith is antagonistic and should be abolished. Who are they to judge someone's faith and do they actually think that they have some kind of divine right to execute a human being? I pray that God is watching their activities and He uses many nations to finally put a stop to ISIS rampage throughout the Middle East. Many world governments and religious leaders have stated that genocide is being committed by ISIS in the Middle East.

In this time in history, many Muslims are converting to Christianity because the way they have been treated at the hands of their own governments and by ISIS. This group is having a reverse effect on the Muslim population converting to Christianity and maybe they don't realize what is happening. When The United Nations and key western nations hear the word genocide, they should all stand-up and take notice as well as take the necessary action. There have been many brutal regimes and butchers in society throughout history and we can't seem to keep them as a part of history. Now once again humanity finds itself in this downward and destructive position.

Chapter 28:

DESTRUCTION OF ARCHAEOLOGICAL STRUCTURES AND SITES

ISIS considers all religious shrines such as Islamic, Christian, Jewish, and others to be idolatrous. ISIS states that the historical objects and sites it destroyed were heresy to its ideology. There are thousands of archaeological sites across Iraq and Syria and some are classified as UNESCO World Heritage sites. The region of Iraq and Syria is considered to be the cradle of life. ISIS destruction of these ancient sites are mostly Muslim archaeological structures. ISIS is selling many of the antiquities to fund their military operations. The reason this group is destroying these archaeological sites is for the purpose of cultural cleansing. Many of these ancient archaeological sites are more than two thousand years old and some people believe the destruction of these sites is a war crime in its own right.

The list of archaeological sites looted, damaged and destroyed by ISIS.

Syria:

Temple of Baalshamin, Palmyra

Temple of Baal, Palmyra

Mar Elian Monastery, al-Qaryatain

Apamea

Dura-Europos

Mari

Iraq:

Hatra, capital of the Parthian Empire

Nineveh, Mosul

Mosul Museum and Libraries

Nimrud, Assyrian City

Khorsabad, Assyrian Palace, Mosul

St. Elijah Monastery, Mosul

Mar Behnam Monastery

Mosque of the Prophet Yunus, Jonah's Tomb, Mosul

Imam Dur Mausoleum, Samarra

This list is from National Geographic and CNN.

Chapter 29:
END OF TIMES-
REVELATIONS

ISIS is envisioning and striving to bring about the apocalypse, the end of times. The only person or entity capable of doing this is God or Jesus. ISIS is understandably irrational if they believe that they can accomplish this feat. Armageddon defiantly won't begin through the hands of ISIS. It is written and it is clear how the end of times will come about. But it is not known when this will happen. Prophecy states that that the final battle will start near the Euphrates River, which runs through Turkey, Syria, and Iraq. ISIS does control many cities along the Euphrates River and this group is paying attention to prophecy.

There is a battle of good against evil happening all around us. Spiritual warfare is taking place on this earth through unseen forces. Many people believe this and many people don't believe. As far as I am concerned ISIS are the Devil's disciples and they certainly behave and act this way. God is paying attention and there will be spiritual repercussions of a great magnitude. Just pay close attention to Jerusalem and as soon as it is threatened a miracle will be seen. The spiritual world is actively roaming on this earth avoiding contact with humans. The day will come when everyone will see clearly and understand.

ISIS does believe that they can cause the apocalypse and start a chain reaction to end life on earth. Why this group wants to do this is beyond imagination. Common sense tells us that they will be responsible for their own demise. There is no logic with this type of attitude and thinking. Maybe this is all about power to control the region around them and to control mankind's destiny. Ultimate control is in the hands of the Almighty and His power is absolute. The Lord of Hosts is watching and His judgment is fair and final.

Chapter 30:
DECAPITATION OF ISIS

The latest information is that Saudi Arabia is going to send aircraft to an airbase in Turkey. Then Saudi Arabia and Turkey together will use their ground forces to attack Syria. It is clear that the Syrian regime of President Assad will be attacked to topple the regime and Saudi Arabia will attack from the south and Turkey will attack from the north. With this possibly happening there will be many different militaries in Syria and the situation will become very fluid and anything could happen. With Russia militarily supporting the Syrian military there could be the possibility of Russian forces attacking the forces of Saudi Arabia and Turkey. Bahrain and The United Arab Emirates (UAE) have already committed to sending in their own ground forces into Syria but have not done so yet.

A proxy war is taking place in Syria with America militarily supporting the Free Syrian Army and the Kurdish Army against the Syrian Army. Apparently soon this proxy war will be expanded with the militaries of Saudi Arabia and Turkey invading Syria to remove President Assad from power. The question is will the Russian military respond and send in their own forces to counterattack to protect President Assad. If that happens will the American military and NATO forces join in and attack the Russian forces. If all of this takes place then this will no longer be a proxy war but a full blown war with two major countries in the world involved. It is inconceivable that this could all happen because it would lead to World War III and a tremendous amount of death and destruction.

If cooler heads don't prevail this could all become reality and in the process, ISIS will be crushed and will not exist anymore. At this time Saudi Arabia is financially supporting ISIS to fight against the Syrian Army. ISIS is a proxy of Saudi Arabia but they aren't effective against the Syrian Army. This is why Saudi Arabia plans to send in their own military to remove President Assad of Syria. Ultimately ISIS will not be tolerated by America and Russia. A plan was put in place to defeat ISIS and it is about to happen. The world will take a breath of relief when ISIS is eliminated and never to be used again for any purpose.